PRAISE FOR JASON RYBERG AND
A SECRET HISTORY OF THE NIGHTTIME WORLD

Welcome to the world of Jason Ryberg—a world of true crimes and misdemeanors in the American grain—transformed through the poet's retelling into miniature works of art. Here's Giuseppe the Billy Goat, the one true and rightful king of a little farm outside Salina, KS, marauding through the gossiping chickens. Here's Grogger the drunk, falling headlong from a porch landing to the pavement below. Here's the ghost of John Brown, his eyes like signal fires, gazing out over a heartland replete with million-dollar mega-farms and mega-churches. "Where god builds a mega church," notes Ryberg, "the devil builds a fireworks / bbq / porn emporium." But he also throws a poet into the mix, sometimes—a poet of witness, loaded up with bad radio and stale coffee, who slows down from a steady cross-country pace to survey the cultural wreckage under "a bright, five-battery-flashlight of a moon."

— **George Wallace**
author of *Smashing Rock and Straight as Razors*
(Blue Light Press 2017)

Reading Ryberg is like driving a pick-up truck across Kansas on shrooms. Jason Ryberg's imagery, as fresh as a midnight S curve, takes the reader on a journey from the city to the wheat fields through a landscape bright with the "five-battery-flashlight of a moon." Forever the Salina cowboy at heart, Ryberg, like a calf roper, lassos the "quicksilver halo of ghost fire," moments deep, spirit-filled with paradox. The poet carries his piggin' string in his teeth, ready to half-hitch a "pint bottle ... to the grinning, blue Buddha moon." He raises both arms into the air and stops the clock.

— **Al Ortolani**
author of *Ghost Sign*
(Spartan Press / 39 West Press 2016)

more ...

Over the last decade, I've returned time and time again to the writing of Jason Ryberg for a lot reasons but mainly because nobody is doing what he does for the Kansas-Missouri literary landscape. He's like a Baptist preacher carrying the weight of forgotten prairies on his able shoulders and dumping their stories on the bar stools of local taverns—just looking for that one great breath of fire. With *A Secret History of the Nighttime World*, he has brought that fire from his heart and put it back on the page.

— **John Dorsey**
author of *Harvey Korman Harvey Korman Harvey Korman*
(Spartan Press 2017)

Beyond the reach of the new-Beats and city lits, Ryberg exists: his writing rattlesnake tough but also tender-hearted as the armored artichoke. What he says will last longer than whiskey breath, oil slick, lemon rind, and a burnt cigarette butt. It will last—as all fine wine and literature does—as long as memory serves.

— **Kevin Rabas**
author of *Songs for My Father*
(Meadowlark 2016)

Jason Ryberg, local boogeyman and snake charmer, writes poetry like a farm boy on shore leave, like a knuckle sandwich from a Klingon preacher, like a reveler after the battle of Canna, like a trouble man on a bender, like an existential Mortimer with the Salina blues, like Charon singing Bukka White to Roy Batty across dark waters they add to with their tears, remembering the smell of cut grass. His lyrics are in argument with the world and in love with his embattled subjects, coming like a last phone call from an uncle on the other side—one who wants to see you wise before the finish line. Formally adept, always fresh, always for real, his poems are masculine, muscular, and tender together and his lyrical voice original and longed for by those of us who know his work. Dig in and dig in now you lucky motherfucker. Do not, at any peril, resist him.

— **Mark Hennessy**
author of *Airport Motel: A Suite for Bad Players*
(Spartan Press 2017)

a secret history of
THE NIGHTTIME WORLD

also by Jason Ryberg

Head Full of Boogeymen / Belly Full of Snakes
(Spartan Press 2016)

Beauty Parlors, Train Yards and Everything In Between
(Spartan Press 2014)

Motel, Diner, Liquor
(Spartan Press 2014)

Down, Down and Away
(Spartan Press 2011)

Blunt Trauma
(Spartan Press 2009)

Open Letter to Dark Gods of the Ancient World
(Unholy Day Press 2004)

Devils, Dice and Car Parts
(Mean and Evil House 2001)

*The Physics of Context:
A Handbook For Outlaws, Exiles and Secret Admirers*
(Mean and Evil House 1994)

Night Sky: Adventures Under the Crushed Velvet Void
(Mean and Evil House 1993)

The Psychedelic Prairie
(Mean and Evil House 1992)

a secret history of
THE NIGHTTIME WORLD

poems (old and new) by
JASON RYBERG

39 WEST

39 WEST PRESS
Kansas City, MO
www.39WestPress.com

39 WEST
PRESS

Copyright © 2017 by Jason Ryberg

All rights reserved. No part of this book may be reproduced, scanned, or distributed in any printed or electronic form, including information storage and retrieval systems, without permission. Please do not participate in or encourage piracy of copyrighted materials in violation of the author's rights. Please purchase only authorized editions.

First Edition: April 2017

ISBN: 978-1-946358-04-2

Library of Congress Control Number: 2017938920

This book is a work of fiction. Names, characters, places, dates, and incidents are products of the author's imagination, or are used fictitiously, satirically, or as parody. Any resemblance to actual persons, living or dead, business establishments, events, or locales is entirely coincidental.

10 9 8 7 6 5 4 3 2

Design, Layout, Edits: Jason Ryberg & j.d.tulloch
Cover Photo: Jeff Hogue
Author Photo: Jon Bidwell

39WP-19

This book is dedicated to
John C. Ryberg, Sr.
and
Melinda T. Husbands Ryberg

CONTENTS

It	3
Dinner with the Devil [Sleight Return]	6
Something to Say	8
Dream #621	10
The Garden of Punishment	11
Dreams of Blue Whales	13
Monday, October 30	15
Bottom Feeders	17
Night Sky	20
Pearl Divers	21
Crushed Velvet Void	22
Whatever *It* Is	24
Madame Laveau, Fortune Teller and Police Psychic, Has a Vision	27
Mr. Grey Skies [Sleight *Redux*]	29
Hotel Dementia	30
Madame Laveau, Fortune Teller and Police Psychic, Falls off the Wagon with a Resounding Thud	33
Mugshots of Lesser Imps and Demons	35
Intimations of Mortality Through a Mad Dog's Eyes (or, Lamar Pye Contemplates, What Could Be, His Last Supper)	37
Blind Dog Barking at a Train	40
Three Blue Tears in a Bucket	42
Jealous Gods, Attorneys General and Cigar Smokin' Monkeys	44
Dream #131-75A: Abandoned Machinery	46

Son of *It*	48
A Little Too Much to Dream Last Night (or, Musta Thought It Was White Boy Day)	50
It's Funny, the Things You Think About, When a Cop Puts a Gun to Your Head	52
Chicken, Matchstick-Man and Unicorn (or, Do Replicants Dream of Suburban Normalcy?)	54
The Gnome in the Corner (or, Pulling Weeds in the Garden of Earthly Delights) [Sleight *Redux*]	58
For Some Reason	59
Loaded Dice and Poisoned Candy	61
What *It* Is (or, That's What I'm Talkin' About!)	63
Everything Gonna Be All Right (or, Trading Body Blows with the Ghost of Victor Smith)	65
Lone Wolves, Black Sheep and Red-Headed Step-Children	67
Psalm #49, from *The Book of Mean and Evil Truths*	69
(Otherwise) Ridiculous	72
Ghosting Around	74
Still-Life with Catfish, James Brown, Dragon and Freight Train	76
And Still the Moon	79
Drunk Directing Traffic at the Intersection of Time and Space	81
Standing at the Intersection of Critical Mass and Event Horizon with Tom Wayne and John Deuser, 5:47am (or, *Hey Man, Is That An Accordion I'm Hearing?*)	83

Charles Simic Sitting in the Cheap Seats of My Dreams	85
Chance Meeting, 3am	87
Madame Laveau, Fortune Teller and Police Psychic, Begins to See the Light	88
Madame Laveau, Fortune Teller and Police Psychic, Hands Out a Little Free Advice	90
The Story, So Far	92
Chet Baker Begins to Bleed	94
Sleep During Thunderstorms	96
Ghost Out Wandering the Backroads (or, John Brown Returns to Kansas)	97
What Else to Do?	99
Midnight on the Eighteenth Hole at the *Club Purgatorio*	101
Head Full of Boogeymen / Belly Full of Snakes (or, No Escape from the Island of Misfit Boyz)	102
Weathervane Creaking in a Sad, Grey Wind (or, a Secret History of the Nighttime World)	105
What Is *It*, This Time?	107
You Are Here: A Meditation on Phenomenology and Spiritualism (with a Side of Jalapeños and Mezcal)	110
Return of *It*	112

Human speech is like a cracked kettle on which we tap crude rhythms for bears to dance to, while we long to make music that will melt the stars.

— Gustave Flaubert

It

It is rumored by the elders of the tribe to reside
somewhere in that mysterious *no-go zone*
on all the ancient sea maps that reads
there be monsters here.

It scratches, kicks and thrashes
in the tunnels beneath our bellies
to remind us we're alive.

It jumps and skitters like dry, dusty leaves
across the cold stone floor of the soul,
sets a spell, then scurries away like a cat
suddenly freed from a back screen door, playing
CATCH ME IF YOU CAN!
CATCH ME IF YOU CAN!

It hangs somewhere off in the distance
of a tall-timer's thousand-yard stare
and routinely sticks a hard one
to the secretary of The Man.

It runs up and down the stairs
in our palatial time-share of many mansions,
a pair of scissors snippity-snipping in each hand.

It gleefully swings from the trees
and sees right through all our best laid plans,
best played hands and meticulously designed destinies.

It pays the rent, pays the tab,
pays the interest (at a healthy 15% I might add),
pays attention, pays it forward, pays it back,
and, if you're lucky (and I mean damn lucky,
like lottery lucky) It'll even play like It gives a damn.

It whispers hope into the ear
of the head that hangs heavy with woe.
It teaches us to speak in ancient tongues
and tongues, ticklishly, the ear
that will not hear the truth.

It revs the search engines
of the chariots of the gods,
idling at inter-net intersections
and high school parking lots
and then *WHOOOOSH,*
It's gone, baby, gone
like a murder of crows
startled into flight by a pack
of *Black Cat* firecrackers
or the *click-clack-BOOM!*
of a random shotgun blast.

Power-lines and playing cards
stuck in bicycle spokes
and pork-pie hats sitting on freshly made beds
are very often vital components of what It is
(as are chairs estranged in dark corners
and hula girls dancing on dashboards, as well):

moonflowers and cirrus clouds,
little red wagons and red, rusted-out wheel barrows,
broken down trains and the ever-reliable
tear-jerking scenario of tears falling somewhere
inside an unexpected summer rain or busted headstones
in forgotten roadside graveyards.

And then there's the snarly, squealy twang
of a pedal-steel guitar and the shriek of cars
firing off the line under the neon /
Mother of Pearl moonlight
on a lonely two-lane highway
somewhere out there this very night.

And of course the big, bad monoliths
of Love, Hate and Madness
are all larger parts of the sum of what It is.

You can map the face of the Earth
with the latest satellite technology,
pick your way, meticulously,
through its gravelly guts,
sift, gingerly, through
the sedimentary layers
of lost civilizations and past lives
and still you grow only colder.

Maybe there's a requisite degree
of desperation or estrangement
to even vaguely perceive the slow-motion,
Matrix-style bullet trail of its passing.

And maybe, before one can rightfully summon It,
one must finally succumb to the hard realization
that they are but a baby lamb
lost in the much-mythologized,
much-poeticized primeval black forest
of the mind,

and the light is falling,

and the crickets and coyotes have ceased
their volleys of calling and responding,

and, is it just me,
or did it just suddenly
get really quiet
out here?

Dinner with the Devil [Sleight Return]

Without so much as a warning, an unwarranted weather-front of attitude is just now swoopin' down; yes, a dark and snarly storm (with roots reaching deep beneath the norm) is about to come biblically floodin' out from some meta-psychic-al steel drum into this tiny china tea-cup of a town.

And the wind is nervously squirming and moaning and pacing around, lookin' for a quiet corner to piss in. And over at the Congo Room (way out there by the tracks), the Stoics are demanding that the Taoists let them pass, but the Taoists are just hangin' ten, man, cuz those guys know when it's all been done and said, neither they nor we nor you nor them ever beats The House: naw man, no one ever really wins (you just hope to cut your losses and call the whole thing even).

And everybody knows (that is, everyone that's in the know), the Devil, he's out there cat-scratchin' somewhere, shuckin' and jivin' and makin' the rounds, hemmin' and hawin' and playin' the clown in the ever-increasingly sinister most interior of a broken-down downtown.

He's rackin' balls and talkin' trash, punchin' tunes and pinchin' ass, tryin' to sniff out a good time or maybe just shadowin' the sidelines, sippin' on a scotch-and-soda, chewin' out a toothy grin.

Yeah, he's rode into town on crow's wings and a cloud of Oklahoma dust and he knows just what to say and do to turn the burner up a touch (beneath a city already close to boiling over with ids and egos and ill-advis'd lusts).

And the wing'd monkeys are circlin', and all your *sources* and *connections* are layin' low, and the cops are all out in force tonight, and the city's fixin' to explode. But, as everybody knows (that is, everyone who's anyone who's even slightly in the know), Taoists never spill their drinks crossin' a crowded room, and if you're gonna dine with the Devil, brothers and sisters, better bring yourself a long motherfuckin' spoon.

Something to Say

Consider a moment
those dank, primeval basements
and mud-flooded sub-basements
of the brain,

where the fish
and lizards
and monkeys
of our formative years
still wriggle and skitter
and scurry about.

If we peer deep enough
inside ourselves
we can see them, there,

still holding the line,
still completing
their respective lengths of circuitry,
still telegraphing up
their two-cents worth,
from time to time,
despite all our attempts
at assimilating and processing them
or even refining them away
down the spiral staircase of the spine.

Look, for example, how the Gar,
with their jagged maniacal grins
are all lustfully eying the little pink toes
of our haplessly bobbing frontal lobe,
while the Catfish are fatly content
to sift and slither in the rich, fertile muck
of prehistoric memory.

And the Skinks and Geckos
and Chameleons,
all contoured and layered together
in their crevices,
are dreaming of the days
when they ran the show.

And the monkeys,
that coffee and smoke-saturated
back-room gaggle
of gag-men and speech writers,
all hunched and contorted
over their cranky old Underwoods,
are up against a bitch of a deadline ...

For the Alpha Male
needs something to say,

something witty and charming,
(yet, still somehow
mysterious and aloof)

and he needs it
yesterday!

Dream #621

Tigers
and dragons
and starfish

(Oh my!),

burning bright
and belching flowers
and tumbling before
my mind's martini-dilated eye.

Goya's grinning donkeys
(and those joyous,
gibbering monkeys)

and the drunken sculptor
we met last week.

Remember that guy
from last Saturday night,

the one you thought
was such
a freak?

The Garden of Punishment

3am
and a bell goes off
somewhere in the dank,
cavernous sub-
sub-basement
of my skull,

sending all the lizards
and crickets
skittering,

signaling
once,
twice,
three times,
that once again
the rich, fertile
sub-terran soil of my soul
is about to host
an after-hours
battle royale.

Here is where
the issues, conundrums
and controversies
of the day are nightly
wrestled, reconfigured
and hammered out.

And at this particular instance
of Insomnolent Half-Dream,
the scenario has assumed the curious
manifestation of a steel-cage match
(complete with razor-wire, cowbells
and kabuki sticks!).

In one corner,
the surly, pissy demon
of Pernicious Debt!

In the other,
the voracious troll
of Conspicuous Consumption!

An audience of Shriners,
nuns and Boy Scouts
howls for blood
and tits!

For they know, they know,

before anyone may enter
the Kingdom of Dreams,

they must first walk
through the Garden
of Punishment.

Dreams of Blue Whales

Tonight the world is wild
with the erotic electro-
pheromonal micro-bursts
of linden trees

and the locusts are really jamming
(though the lone cricket
clicks and chirps
in horny, sorrowful longing)

and God's good eye is beaming
its silvery, mystical spotlight,
center-stage, down through the hole
torn in the top
of the dark circus tent
of clouds.

So, here's where we find
our bold (and here-to-for
missing) mis-adventurers,

sleeping out in the backyard,
so carefully and conspicuously arranged
amongst this atmospheric nocturne
of fireflies and empty beer cans,
moonflowers and Marigolds
and giggling garden gnomes:

a circle of narcoleptic
synchronized swimmers,

slowly
spiraling
down

through
layer
after churning,
swirling
oceanic
layer

into
the deep
undulant dreams
of blue whales.

Monday, October 30

That cold-blooded bastard, the wind,
is having his way with
the house tonight

while some surly, third-rate deity
is dragging a dark blanket
of clouds over the city.

The gnarled and spidery trees all
rattle and creak like Halloween's
cracked and splintered bones

and the crows
have folded up their
feathers for the day,

morphing into
the slippery black shadows
of early evening.

So, Old Man Winter has just now decided
to send his heralds and representatives
in across the state line,

each one trailing
long flowing banners like haunted
rivers of gray weather.

And once again
the good people of Kansas have been
caught with their short pants on;

for the wind, the clouds,
the trees, the crows;
they are telling us

that school is officially *in session*
and that our love for each other
will be tested.

Bottom Feeders

The ghosts of old dreams
are washed out video-shadows
milling about in salvage stores,
train yards and vacant lots,
muttering state secrets
and family recipes into the wind.

The ghosts of old dreams
are fleeting quicksilver gleams
in the corner of the mind's eye,
and then, suddenly,
in a flurry of back road dust
and magpie wings,
are smoke.

The ghosts of old dreams
are fat bottom feeders, much like
their not-so-distant cousin the catfish.

In fact, they often dine
at the same greasy spoons
and bed down at the same
flophouse hotels …

a hollow log, a tire, a Christmas tree,
(a chamber in the heart,
a cavern in the skull),

maybe a washer or refrigerator, whatever,
wherever there's a vacancy
or a free meal.

They do what they can to survive.

It has been said
that there is a giant catfish
somewhere at the bottom of the world:

bigger than the blue whale,
huger than the ever-meditative brontosaurus,
more gigantic, even, than the ancient,
fabled leviathan that still haunts the sleep
of poets and deep sea divers, alike.

And many believe
this surly old boy to be god —

way down deep there
among the jutting pillars
and slowly eroding walls
and steel skeletons
of his first clumsy experiments
with civilization,

slithering and sucking about,
sifting and breathing out our days
from the primal mud and muck of life,

accompanied only
by his angelic battalions of advisers,
his armored corps of engineers,
the crawdads.

And look,
there they are,
rippling out around him
in concentric circles
and billowing coronas of silt,
hard at work,
sniffing,
tasting,

testing,
triangulating,

picking, meticulously, over the tiny,
time-filtered bits and pieces of the past,
reworking the problems of the world
from the bottom up.

It has also been said
that no other creature of his creation
can withstand such depths,

except perhaps
(if you believe in such things),

the ghosts of old dreams.

Night Sky

The night sky stretches out above us
like the hide of some dark leviathan,
flayed and pulled taut on stakes like a circus tent,
the angry, purple-black bruises of clouds
slowly dispersing, moving on towards
Topeka, Abilene, Salina, Dodge …
to feed the lonely fitful sleep of outlaws,
exiles and secret admirers everywhere.

Bathed in the blue liquid light
of the night sky, we are soon reduced
to those things most immediate,
maybe even, most urgent:
the cold, flapping curtains of mist,
the snaky twist and hiss of tall grass,
the oily flow of red wine, wood smoke
and rainwater over our tongues.

All the little conversations have stopped,
the tracks of their sentences leading
to the edge of a dark, thoughtless gulf.
Coyotes and crows, field-mice and hitch-hikers,
the ghosts of old pioneers, even; everyone
pausing to listen, faces turned up, to the distant,
musical crank and groan of gears and engines …
the solar system turning on its axis.

Pearl Divers

We've crossed two states to be here
on this shiny, blue Saturday afternoon
of hot cosmic winds and A.M. radio crackle,
chrome, clouds and melting tarmac,
eye to eye with ears of corn,
drunk on beer and pollen.

And way over there, on the side of the road,
is the *U.S.S. Chevrolet,* looking like it's been
run aground and abandoned somewhere
off the coast of what surely must be Nebraska
(the captain and crew very possibly searching
for native girls or scavenging for food).

Yes, here we are, sifting through someone's cornfield,
as if we were pearl divers, perhaps, diving capped
and flippered, swimming in a sea of yellow and green
(confessing our sins to crows as we go) recalling again
and again what surely must have been an ancient
Chinese maxim, *that a man's soul is a pearl.*

Everywhere around us is the sound of the friction
of the wind filtering through this field of tall corn,
an all-encompassing hiss like the electric crackle
of static, haunted with distant whispering or the dry,
dusty rustling of a million newspapers
that read nothing but old news.

Crushed Velvet Void

The world has drawn back its billowed drapes
and here we stand on the blurred edge of evening,
our thoughts telescoping light years
towards some dark, distant point.

Stretching, on the very tips
of our twinkling, naked toes,
we reach for escape velocity
and with one massive explosion of effort
we leap into the turning sky,
tucking, rolling and tumbling
into the soft, layered darkness
of the crushed velvet void.

Suddenly the Earth is a small glass bead
or an unblinking eye, swirling with cataracts
of weather and civilization.

There, to our right,
spanning the great expanse
of the chemical / color spectrum,
are the star factories:
cirrus and stratocumulus clouds
of glowing gas and glittering dust,
slowly contracting, condensing
into clusters of fertile ground
which will one day give rise to flowering suns
and the smoking seeds of planets.

It has been said
that the universe was once held
to be a giant egg shell,
flecked and speckled with
millions of holes through which shined
the divine light of heaven,

so that the gods might monitor
our progression,
our evolution,
our gestation ...

But we,
with all our modern conventions
and standard models of wisdom,
have come to see the universe
in a different light,

a brilliant showering of sparks
to show us the way.

Whatever *It* Is
for Tom Wayne

Whether It's the iron will
of the invisible, all-seeing, all-knowing football coach /
prison warden / stern, but lovable, grandpa
with magical powers that lives in the sky
or the slightest whim of the Almighty Illuminati,

the icy fingers of cosmic / Karmic irony
(probing the tender nether-regions
of your mind), or, the very *moment*
of which so many speak, so many advise,
so many so earnestly poeticize;

that last, final, indivisible *whatever* ...

Maybe this time thinly disguised
as a perfectly common word
in a book on Lipizzaner ponies
(or Japanese Bonsai trees)
found at a Goodwill store
in downtown Norman, OK:

a word you're absolutely sure you know you know
(or, know you once knew, anyway, maybe in some
past life scenario, at least) but now seems to have
stripped its gears, dislodged itself and fallen right out
of the basic machinery of regular usage and instant
recognition all together, forcing you to re-evaluate
your mutual non-aggression pact with all words.

Or, maybe It's a praying mantis, eyeballing you,
inquisitively, from your sleeve,
lightning shattering a night sky, again and again,
like a giant sheet of windshield glass,

a fortune cookie with no fortune in it,
or a fireworks stand that, upon closer examination,
turns out to be a small island oasis
of Mexican summer dresses.

Or, a car horn firing once
and then some overly precocious little kid
(your nephew or second cousin, let's say)
announcing, suddenly (and, to no one
in particular, by which we can also mean
to any- or everyone in the world),

E, definitely the key of E.

Or, maybe It's just a single sweat bee
lazily *perning* and *gyring* above a perfectly poured
and pristine pint of Guinness, currently sitting
on a cafe table in the sun ... whatever.

For many, a myth or, at best,
something one waits around for
like a cab in a bad part of town
or a sign from one of the many
One True Gods (of your choice).

For others, It is the object
of the ever-vigilant votive candle in the window.

And once again, It has come upon you, stealthily,
in a state of indecision, disorientation or bad faith
like a payphone ringing (with vaguely ominous intent)
by the side of a two-lane desert highway,

or a postcard sent a long time ago
from someone you haven't thought about in years,
found in a book you always meant to finish (hiding
for who knows how long under the couch),

or, as a ruggedly Hollywood-handsome man,
suddenly materializing before you,
claiming to be a U.S. federal marshal, and who,
it seems, is attempting to serve you *papers*
of some variety or another with a distant, empty stare
that conveys, somehow,

that this was not, at all,
what he ever thought
he'd be doing with the prime
crime-fighting,
door-kicking,
terror-plot-thwarting
years of his life.

Oh well.

Whatever.

Madame Laveau, Fortune Teller and Police Psychic, Has a Vision

And this time,
for some reason,
there's a Charlie Chaplin of a scarecrow
standing in the middle of a crossroads,
staring, blankly, up at the sky, arms outstretched
with a pipe-bomb in one hand
and a bottle of Pernod in the other.

And the sky itself is a living, breathing,
billowing fishnet of a tapestry woven of starfish
and moonflowers, star fruit and banana peppers
and little jade lions with smiles
as wide as the seas of time.

In the bottom right corner of the scene,
there's a pile of rictus-ly grinning carnival masks
blooming with cherry blossoms
and someone's spare change
(some kind of foreign currency, it seems).

And just to the right of that (and down a little),
we can see your classic *hoary country preacher-type,*
with a rainbow variety of snakes crawling from his
pockets and sleeves, shirt-collar and pant legs,
staggering his way towards his unsuspecting flock
(not shown here).

And, just a few years from this very spot,
there's a hobo clown with a hernia
and a stove-pipe hat,
smoking a clove cigarette
and sipping, solemnly,
from a bottle of Applejack.

And he's sitting atop an aging rhinoceros
(that, by the way, is just about to do its *business*
from a steel I-beam, thirteen floors up
on a swaying skeletal structure
which, the locals say, will one day be
the *federal memorial something-or-other*
dedicated to *some fancy so-and-so*).

And, finally, there in the background,
just behind (and up to the left)
of the Night Blooming Cereus,

if one squints hard enough
(as if peering into a painting by van Eyck
or maybe one of those *Where's Waldo* dioramas),

one can almost see it ...

Life, itself (portrayed here
in some vague, anthropomorphic
manifestation), lurking unnervingly
beneath the pale orange glow of the streetlamp
and the churning cloud of Death's-Head Moths.

Mr. Grey Skies [Sleight *Redux*]

Don't you come around here, no more, Mr. Grey Skies, Mr. No-Heart-And-All-Lies, Mr. Fork'd-Tongue-And-Snak'd-Eyes, with your no-more tomorrows and your low-down tonights, your goat's feet and your crow's wings and your icicle-daggers always refracting a, somehow, unnatural light, your gibbering devil-monkeys and third-rate conspiracies and your spindly spider-web dreams spinning from the fat, under-belly of night. No one wants to see your cockroach of a heart pinned to your sleeve. No one wants to smell the unhealthy funk of your ragman's bag of miseries. No one here wants anything to do with what you got to offer, Mr. Black Hand Man. So, get your shit-house rats and your loaded dice, your hangman's noose and your butcher's knife, then, take two steps back and turn away, turn away, turn away from the river of life (in which you may never, ever again step twice). Now go get your shine-box, boy, pack your bags and PUT THE GLASS DICK DOWN! Go wait shamefully at the station (with a dumb look on your face) for the last bus out of town. And you best not be seen creepin' 'round here no more you dirty little whore, Mr. Grey Skies, Mr. River-Of-Tears-And-Halo-Of-Flies, Mr. Keep-A-Man-Down-No-Matter-How-Hard-He-Tries. *No-sir-ee,* Stagger Lee, from this day forth I break with thee, I break with thee, I break with thee. I reclaim the body, mind and soul that I once mortgaged to thee. I spit fire at your cold fish's eye. I kick hot sand at your sly gargoyle face. I kick dog shit on your fancy shoes. Not one more time will I hand over my money and my keys to you. Not one more time will I sacrifice my precious time for you. Not one more time will I follow you like a little, lost lamb or a red-headed stepchild into your forest of black, creaking skeletons. Now take it on the heel-and-toe, motherfucker, before I whack ya one!

Hotel Dementia

Well, the foreign ambassadors
have finally arrived
and the early evening sky is wellin' up
and threatenin' to unload
its whole rag-bag repertoire
of woeful confessional poems.

And the heiress in the lobby
is channeling Nefertiti's hairdresser
and the orthopedic shoe salesman
from Sheboygan is playin' Russian roulette
with a juicy piece of jailbait from *somewhere
down South* and his uncle Pico's .38.

And the front desk clerk
is desperately searching for a vein
and the ladies bridge club is hopelessly pixelated
and the Siamese twin bellhops (from Bulgaria, no less)
are furiously bickering, non-stop (Jesus, what a mess),
over the proper split on a skinny tip from
a second-rate rock star's third-rate groupie.

And it looks like the clown in the hermitage
is nursing a hernia and the Moonies are kickin' it
old school out in the courtyard,
and the shriners are already swashbuckling drunk
and bum-rushing the ballroom, hoping to catch
Miss Lily Lafontaine's *big finale*.

And the monkeys are getting restless
and the management is clearly negligent
and the mad scientist with the bad rug
and the ridiculous accent
is down in his makeshift lab,

trying to graft bat wings, a lizard's tail
and a nine-volt battery
to a giant habanera, mumbling
Mad!? I'll show zem who's mad!

And down the secret staircase in the back,
the hotel detective is in hot pursuit
of a giggling ghost woven of calliope tunes,
old dreams and clove cigarette smoke (and,
suspected of cold-bloodedly
short-sheeting all the beds).

And the Chinese acrobats are shooting craps
and standing on their heads in the presidential suite
(while sipping a supernatural tea made of mandrake,
purple hyacinth and dragonfly wings).

And now the chef is raising hell
and all the Mexicans are screaming,
the golem is getting' twitchy (the gargoyles,
a little bitchy) and the poet on the thirteenth floor
is foolishly attempting to breed newspaper tigers
with tinfoil unicorns, his mother pounding and
pounding on the adjoining door,
horrified at the sounds she's hearing.

But, at least the hit man is dreaming, sweetly,
of brown-skin girls and fancy boat drinks
and the nightclub singer is rehearsing
his (or is it her?) routines
in front of a cracked funhouse mirror.

And the smoldering gypsy-prince
(always napping in the pantry)
is conjuring sinister hexes
with which to whither the rival man-roots
of all the other *mules* in the *stall*,

leaving their women desperate
and defenseless before him.

And way up in the attic
the colonel is orchestrating a grand battle at sea
in an ancient cast-iron tub,
and the sniper up their with him
is making outrageous demands for chicken wings
and pink champagne, and the bodies long buried
under the boiler room floor have finally become
fed up with all the noise.

And all the lights begin to flicker
and the walls start to bleed Chambord
and books and magazines
begin to flap around the rooms
and the place is really hoppin' now
and there's no *cap'm* at the helm
and the weather's finally jumpin' down
with both No. 13 feet.

And the triple-headed hellhounds have been released
and the wing'd horses all set free
and there you find yourself, inexplicably,

standing in the men's room,
the exact same time every goddamn night
for the last … who knows how many years …

a dumb look on your face,
a carnival mask in your hand,
an intensely dapper chap telling you,

You're the maintenance man.

You've always been the maintenance man.

Madame Laveau, Fortune Teller and Police Psychic, Falls off the Wagon with a Resounding Thud

I see a dark and cluttered curiosities shop
overflowing with old tuxedos and fancy combs,
snuff boxes and porcelain china dolls,
big belt buckles and giggling garden gnomes,
books and magazines and postcards from places
that no longer exist (addressed to people
who've been dead for decades).

And now a sleeping woman wafting along
past the store-front window as if carried
by invisible wings that only unfold when she dreams.

I see an ominous Gothic architecture
full of monstrous ideas (stuffed
and mounted, but still not quite dead).

I see an old, run-down vaudeville theater
where-in old, run-down drunks and junkies
watch naked emotions writhe and gyrate
upon a spot-lit stage.

I see leaves falling on the surface of a pond:
fish bones, beer bottles, rowboats
and the ghosts of old hobos asleep on the cold,
muddy bottom.

I see a plow mule, trapped and maddened,
in the ballroom of an abandoned antebellum mansion,
and a furious black thunderstorm (with lightning
in its hair) pounding and pounding at the front door,
demanding offerings of spare change
and *Chateauneuf du Pape.*

I see a sailor in a bar,
drinking gin and playing gin rummy
(secretly pining for his past life as a barn swallow),
and a tailor's dummy standing in the corner
of a tiny room, just upstairs from the bar,
the soles of somebody's shoes showing
from beneath the bed, something sinister or ridiculous
(or both) about to happen.

I see a man shuffling down a dark street,
unable to sleep without his nightly dosage
of Ellington's *Indigos* or Gould's *Variations*.

His heart is a wasp's nest laboring
earnestly to make honey.
His head is a hotel kitchen
full of screaming Greeks and Mexicans and Slavs,
(and, one lost and rather simple looking white boy).

The man has stooped to pick something up
from the street corner, an important-looking key
on a bright red string,
a Christmas ornament, almost,
in its shining, ornate delicacy.

Though he will later misplace it
somewhere foolishly obvious
during some minor but rollicking misadventure
involving a plumber and a midget transvestite
(or maybe a mega-church minister
and a one-legged ballerina?);

never the less, it will continue to lead him
in ever-widening and shrinking circles
like an ill-advised obsession or broken divining rod.

Most likely for the rest of his life.

Mugshots of Lesser Imps and Demons

This one appears regularly
under crescent moons,
sitting on rickety bridges,
sipping on a forty of menthol-flavored Colt-45.
However, sometimes, it will be found
wandering about the back roads,
looking for a ride into town.
Halfway there it will disappear.

This one sleeps in the trunk of a Gran Torino
with no wheels, abandoned in a vacant lot
behind an anarchist bookstore in Cleveland, OH.
Its favorite composer is Mahler.
Its favorite flower is the Marigold.

This one will occasionally call at odd hours,
asking for people who no longer live there.
However, it will insist on speaking to them anyway.

This one says nothing but hums, inanely,
and smells, faintly, of honeysuckle and blackpowder.

This one routinely appears at the scenes
of fallen elevators and speedboat wrecks,
eyes put out with BBs, grease fires
and accidents caused by running with scissors.

This one can often be heard cackling, madly,
late at night and lives, exclusively,
on a diet of pink champagne and fortune cookies.

This one will appear, mysteriously, in old photographs
with kings, presidents and various other dignitaries
(and, more often than not, wearing a ridiculous hat).

This one rises each night from the bottom of a pond
to pinch babies and steal car keys.
It's official title is *Sower of Discord*.

This one lives under the stairs
in the boiler-room of an abandoned
insane asylum in Buffalo, NY.
With the proper rituals and offerings,
it has been known to provide alcohol for minors
and false identification for people on the lam.

This one rides through the storm-grey skies
of nightmares on the wings of Magpies
or clinging to the fur of house-flies
wafting on currents of cross-winds.

This one throws dice every Saturday night
in the basement of a half-way house for fallen angels.
His super-powers and origin are unknown.

All of them remain *at-large*.

None of them will ever give you a straight answer.

Intimations of Mortality Through a Mad Dog's Eyes (or, Lamar Pye Contemplates, What Could Be, His Last Supper)

Through a mad dog's eyes,
the right subtle shift in perception,
like the tumble and click of a combination lock
or secret code or complex equation,
suddenly fathomed at 3 or 4am, maybe,
can bring you to your bended knees
on the cold flower-patterned linoleum
of God's dungeon floor.

Soon you find yourself there, nightly,
supplicant and luridly genuflected
before the smooth, round ass of Lady Death,
(of which, it is rumored, tastes faintly
of French Vanilla, Mimosa and black powder).

Looking through a mad dog's eyes,
one can even come to admire
the legendary phantom sniper
(your long-lost evil twin, perhaps) who
has suddenly begun to appear, everywhere:

on rooftops and overpasses and grassy knolls ,
in the backseats of unmarked cars,
in the cruxes of the tallest trees
and 'round every other corner
in the corners of your eyes.

It is whispered among the elders of the tribe
that he's put many a mad dog into a shallow grave,
and lately, the tiny mosquito frequency of his cross hairs
has been tickling your ears and purring, incessantly,
around your sweaty furrowed brow.

But, meanwhile,
just outside of town,
all the bloodshot TV-eyes
are turning away from the senator's aide
and the half-naked cheerleader
who are being pulled from the lake,
and the cops are all out raking the cornfield
with hounds teeth and itchy trigger fingers,

hoping to find a trace
of the raggedy, rangy scarecrow of a man
with the nail in his foot and a bullet in his side.

But, we all know it's *you*.
You're the one.

And you're just *kickin' it,*
sittin' inside your Naugahyde booth
in the diner by the side of the road,
takin' it all in from the big-screen picture window.

And they're comin', boy,
they're comin' for you.

They're lookin' for somebody's crazy uncle,
somebody's low-down, good-for-nothin' son,
somebody's shit-head brother-in-law,
written off for dead ten years ago —
one more dirty white boy
that no one but his mama could ever love.

But she died.

Yeah, that's right, this has been just another sad
cocaine / Cadillac cowboy song
about one more unwanted lone wolf / black sheep /
red-headed, hair-lipped step-child of God,

who got tired after all the years
of trying to tell the old man what he wanted to hear,

tired of tryin' to do the right thing
and always getting' it thrown back
in your face all wrong,
tired of tryin' so damn hard to be good
when the world just begs you to be bad.

And there he is, boys,
just sittin' there,
beamin' out a wounded tiger's smile,
pickin' the last little bits of his last meal
from his fearsome teeth
with a thorn.

Blind Dog Barking at a Train

There's a blind dog barkin' at a train,
a bloodhound with the broke-dick blues,
a scarecrow standin' at a crossroads,
a radio cryin' in a one-hour room,
a radio cryin' in a one-hour room.

There's a moth circling the porch light,
there's a jackalope on the hill,
there's a sad boy prayin' for his luck to change
but he knows it never will, Lord,
he knows it never will.

There's a ghost out wanderin' the back roads
and two mules kickin' where there should be one,
there's a stud-bull rubbin' up against the barb-wire
and a mean boy lookin' for his gun, Lord,
a mean boy lookin' for his gun.

There's a preacher shittin' in the backwoods,
there's a senator pissin' in the wind,
there's a poet in the graveyard
whistlin' *Dixie* in the dark
and something creepin' up behind him,
something creepin' up behind him.

There's roosters crossed with hoot-owls
crossed with crickets crossed with stars,
and blind bats flappin' in the attic
and black cats scratchin' in the barn,
wayward sons gone for months now
and mamas done worryin' where they are.

There's a statue of a little kid
pointing where the money's hid.
There's bones in the trunk of a car,
bones in the trunk of a car.

There's a blind dog barkin' at a train,
there's a drunk man laughin'
at a silver dollar moon,
there's a convict crawlin' through a cornfield,
there's a record skippin' in a lonely room,
a record skippin' in a lonely room.

Saints, outlaws and street cleaners,
eagles, earthworms and butterflies
big shots, bagmen and nobodies,
you better know it happens to everybody:
No matter how I struggle and strive,
I'll never get outta this world alive,
I'll never get outta this world alive,
I'll never get outta this world alive ...

Three Blue Tears in a Bucket

Three blue tears in a bucket,
a river of tears in the rain,
a treehouse fallin' in the back-woods,
a blind dog barkin' at a train,
a blind dog barkin' at a train.

A dead man watchin' soap operas,
a beer bottle moanin' with the wind,
a girl in black waitin' at the Amtrak station
never to be seen again,
never to be seen again.

Three blue tears in a bucket,
a broken down truck stuck in the weeds,
a world of good intentions versus
a thimble-full of bad dreams, Lord,
a thimble-full of bad dreams.

A bleeding Jesus on the dashboard,
a bathtub Virgin for a shallow grave,
a rock that's dripping honey,
a mattress stuffed with money,
a house gone up in flames,
Lord, a house gone up in flames.

Three blue tears in a bucket,
a weathervane creakin' in a sad grey wind,
a whole closet full of skeletons
and a belly full of gin,
a belly full of gin.

Three blue tears in a bucket,
a river of tears in the rain,
a needle full of white light,
a little *save the baby* to ease the pain.
Three blue tears in a bucket
the Lord won't take you but you wish he would,
three blue tears in a bucket
all your cryin' aint gonna do you no good,
no, your cryin' aint gonna do you no good,
your cryin' aint gonna do you no good,
no, your cryin' aint gonna do you no good.

Jealous Gods, Attorneys General and Cigar Smokin' Monkeys

Thirteen Mexican blackbirds who've burst from a pie,
flittering and skittering, nervously, about the scene.

Thirteen devils dancing on the head of a ten-penny nail,
driven into the skull of a snitch.

A bear in a sundress sipping fine Darjeeling
and reading Rabelais
and a bull consulting the *I Ching*
(each keeping a wary eye on the other
from opposite ends of the room).

A surgeon juggling bone saws and whistling show tunes.

A bloodhound with the boot-ass blues,
a skeleton with a fool's cap
and a blind swordsman folding origami cranes.

3 Elvises eating chicken wings and playin' spades
and a vampire sipping cappuccino,
smoking cigarillos and reading yesterday's USA Today.

A grand master of the Drunken Monkey Technique
precariously balanced on the back of a chair and
a teary-eyed clown with a fierce and elaborate network
of girdles and trusses, holding a single red rose,
sitting atop a unicorn.

A lawyer centering her chakra and a lounge-singer
finding his power-animal (most likely a mountain lion
or salamander or maybe even a raven with a cigarette
in its beak).

A cheerleader purging behind a dumpster,
a preacher on the verge of kicking out
a stained glass window
and a circus-midget's smirking ghost,
skulking under a bloody moon.

A jealous god sulking on top of Mt. Fuji,
contemplating the weather and whether
to smite Mr. Jones with a suitcase full of money
or enlighten Mr. Brown with a falling baby grand.

An attorney general holed up in his secret fortress
at the bottom of Lake Wazzapamani, plotting
random harassments and senseless acts of patriotism.

And, finally, beneath the massively Gothic
Masonic temple, in downtown Salina, Kansas,
in the hermetically sealed obscurity
of sub, sub-basement #3,
a hundred cigar-smokin' monkeys
are sitting at their big Macs and fancy PCs,
staring blankly at the blank, glowing screens …

waiting
                    waiting
                                      waiting.

Dream #131-75A: Abandoned Machinery

Here we are
down among the weeds
and slime and stones;

no Davey Jones lockbox
of jewels and pearls and Spanish *doubloons*
to be found down here but

maybe a bicycle and some beer bottles,
an old water-heater and a Christmas tree,
a refrigerator, a rowboat
and a tire or two.

And only moments before
our eyes were sleepily blinking away
the blustery winter-blue fuzz
of early, early morning TV.

But now we've opened them
to find ourselves *waaaay* in over our heads
in this ghostly chartreuse translucence
with only the faint, frayed hems
of shimmering curtains of light
to illuminate the way,

and nothing but you and me
and this languidly churning
underworld around us ...

But, hold on a second,
what's this, here,
way down
at the bottom
of what we always believed

to be just another old
flooded-out gravel pit
in the middle of Kansas?

A lost city, maybe,
or an ancient Martian outpost,
long-abandoned, even
before man walked upright?

Hell, who knows,
now, it's a home only
to catfish and crawdads

and the shadows of lost
or merely *decommissioned* dreams.

Son of *It*

Sometimes It comes to us
early in the morning,
just before the Boss Man turns on the big light,
or in the middle of the saddest,
most haunted part of night:

some kind of slavering,
black behemoth, from what little we can see:
all teeth, tusks and talons,
snuffle and snarl
and primal, predatory aura.

A lonesome and sorrowful thing,
that looks to be part wombat,
swamp gator and slithering bottom-dweller,
mandrill, bloodhound, wild boar
and raging woolly mammoth,

as well as something distinctly ...

other.

Sometimes it batters at the gates
of my brain with its great paws
and its battering ram of a skull
like the giant fist of an angry
underworld god, shaking the walls
of this remote, little city-state of mind.

Sometimes It just rubs its back up against
the great tree trunk of my spine,
thrumming and thrumming
with what surely must be the funky frequency
of warm fuzzy love,

or, at the very least, the manic need
to satisfy some maddening metaphysical itch
(his or mine, I'm never sure).

And, sometimes
It's content to merely loiter
and look on, inquisitively,
studying our most insignificant routines
from just inside the tree line,
just beyond the reach
of our guard lights,

nothing but your classic *dark silhouette*
and *glowing set of eyes* ...

But, of course, it could never really
charge out of that dark forest
of the wild night world of the soul,
and, by some freak cosmic occurrence
of a just and loving god blinking
or even looking the other way,
make its way into our safe, little,
climate-controlled environment.

Could it?

A Little Too Much to Dream Last Night
(or, Musta Thought It Was White Boy Day)
with apologies to The Electric Prunes, Quentin Tarantino and Lawrence Ferlinghetti

She
    with the ab-SO-lutely hypnotic,
                interstellar-black hair
        and maliciously exposed mid-riff

(meaning that radioactive area between,
                but also including,
    upper-most hip bone
        and lower-most rib)
                        asked me to stay
      past last call, promising

    to spirit me away
        from it all (meaning, I suppose,
my otherwise meaningless life
            of de-meaning, semi-skilled toil
      and celibate drudgery)
                to some as yet undisclosed,
but no doubt, exotic locale
        for a volatile psycho /
    sexual concoction which she guaranteed
would be equal parts intensive research

      into the depths of human depravity

and dogged dedication to exhausting
            my mental,
                    physical and
                          moral reserves.

Whereupon, I immediately snorted awake,
                      hours later,

sprawled Golgotha-like
            on my living room floor,
my moment of truth
            too good to be anything but
                        a cruel, booze-fueled dream,
    an alcoholic alien abduction
                leaving me bedraggled
                and discombobulated in its wake,
                            wearing nothing but
a t-shirt and a single black sock (with
            big toe protruding through
                    as if to say
                            hellloooooo),

    front door and fridge wide open,
                every light in the house on
                                and blazing
            like a mid-day desert sun,

        one hand clamped on some kind of
                suspicious looking Dagwood sandwich,
    the other around a half-full beer,

a movie blaring out
            into the early morning dark

    for all the good people
            of the neighborhood to hear,
    someone sinister saying,

                    *shiiit, he musta thought
                            it was white boy day.*
    It aint white boy day, is it?

            *Naw, man,
                    it aint white boy day.*

It's Funny, the Things You Think About, When a Cop Puts a Gun to Your Head

The wings of jungle birds
and butterflies the size of catcher's mitts,
fluttering and flapping all around me
in this dream I once had where
I'm standing in a clearing in the middle
of some jungle, somewhere, beneath a sky
like a giant cut glass punch bowl
or classically Ptolemaic crystal sphere,
the sun, the clouds, the stars and moon,
each fixed in their proper place
in the grand arrangement of things,
all rolling, mechanically, over me,
down and under, back up and over, again and again.

The wind like summer's own breath smelling faintly
of cut grass, chlorine and coconut oil (no other
collusion of smells so mutually and perfectly
complimentary for pulling up so many memories,
so much of that deep down, body and soul type ache
from so far down in the well).

Or, that time Tato and I drove a load
of antique furniture to Neah Bay, WA
(the northwestern-most point of the U.S.,
by the way) and it's storming, off and on,
all the way along this winding two-lane coastal road,

and the wind is beating the crap out of the truck,
and the rain is beading on the windshield
like Diamels or broken strings of costume jewelry,
refracting the headlights of on-coming cars
into a million tiny rays, the preacher on the radio
shouting *for I am the light, I am the way!*

The dark, silent guestroom
of your compounding absence
collapsing ever-inwards upon its
no-thing-ness, its just-not-there-ness
ever since you skipped town that day.
Jesus, has it been two summers, already?
Where were you, when I needed you, baby?
What are you doing these days and is he or she
(whoever they are) keeping you happy?

And, for some reason ... stones
(somehow like the skulls of sad, hobo clowns
who dreamed, foolishly, of being poets,
of all things) sleeping underground,
now and forevermore, through the slow
rotation of the seasons.

Do they still dream down there and if so,
what do they dream of (now and forevermore,
or, until some supreme being (or next closest thing)
finally decides to stop the whole show,
in much the same way, maybe, that someone
might put a gun to someone else's head)?

Down there beneath a thick blanket of snow
and a sheet of leaves, down there beneath the soles
of my and this cop's shoes and the cold, unfeeling glare
of a phosphorescent moon, tangled up among
the roots of Winter's bony, bloodless trees
where their mothers will never find them.

Chicken, Matchstick-Man and Unicorn (or, Do Replicants Dream of Suburban Normalcy?)

You have suddenly returned
from another strange
foreign film of a dream
(of a life of suburban normalcy,
of all things)

only to find yourself (this time)
to be the sole proprietor of an illegal speak-easy,
an elegant bar in a haunted hotel
or maybe a swank nightclub in some exotic
Middle-Eastern city.

There's the grinning ghost of a bartender,
the dapper phantom of a waiter,
the wise and loyal door-man
and the lone customer (slowly
being lowered by unseen forces
down into the bottomless well
of alcohol and madness).

In the back room
an unmanned projector
is playing the same dirty movie
over and over (the old, silent one
with all the really good parts cut out).

Maybe an idealistic, young poet
or fearless and fabulously handsome
and urbane leader of some underground
resistance movement (or some other type
of martyr to lost causes) is hiding out
in one of the empty rooms upstairs

(maybe even the one where the *unfortunate incident*
occurred last year) while someone (or thing)
even more unsettling sleeps in the basement
during the days.

You cater to an elite demographic of socialites,
sociopaths and wiseguy-wannabes,
old-school drunkards and new world samurai,
art school Muppets and indie-rock sock monkeys,
and your only real competition is a dance club
across the street, run by a shady pair of demons
named *Scratchmo* and *Sniffy*.

And it's way into the afterhours now
and you're the only one still around
and you're deep into a bottle of grappe or chartreuse
(or some other variant of industrial-strength
cleaning product).

And over in the corner, a player piano
clankity-clanks away on some ancient,
unrecognizable echo of a tune.

And the moon is peering in at you
and someone has been leaving you
strange little anonymous gifts —

a tiny chicken made from a chewing gum wrapper,
a man whittled from a single Blue Tip match
and a unicorn folded from a receipt
for Chinese takeout,

an origami unicorn that, for some reason,
seems to be more than just
an origami unicorn.

So, who is it, exactly, you've
stayed up this late waiting for, tonight
and every night, for who knows how long?

Surely not that smoky,
back roads cat of a gypsy girl,
to suddenly come calling?

Or your oldest, brightest flame, maybe,
to finally come crawling back to you
through all the highway wreckage of the years?

Or maybe you're waiting
(along with all the other sad-sack chumps out there)
on some messiah type character
or mystified guru dude to make some kind
of big budget Hollywood entrance
with the keys to Shiva's hoopty in one hand
and the teacher's edition of *Life's Big Book
of Mysteries* in the other (you know, the one
with all the answers in the back).

Or maybe it's the legendary
Witness Relocation Man
and his elite tactical unit
of make-over and clean-up technicians
coming to spirit you away
to your new identity,
your newly re-revised history,
your brand new life, overflowing
with excitement and adventure,
complete with spotless credit report
and complimentary suitcase full of cash,
personal trainer,
new car,
new house,
new face,

perfect teeth,
perfect chest,
perfect bi-ceps,
more hair,
more time,
more life?

Not likely.

The Gnome in the Corner
(or, Pulling Weeds in the Garden
of Earthly Delights) [Sleight *Redux*]

Here, inside the wire-mesh margins of the lush, overflowing Garden of Earthly Delights, one has to wonder, sometimes, whether there can possibly be a more maddeningly torturous plight (albeit, of the more gardenly varietal type) than finding yourself in over your head in a little social terrarium full of burstingly ripe nymphs and naiads, who, no matter what you say or do, cannot hear or see or, in some other way, get a feel for you, *or*, those very same nymphs and naiads very obviously in the company of various garden variety sorts of newly-moneyed new world orderlies and alpha white knights and future provider-types that, in every conceivable way, appear to be the very antithesis of you. And you know exactly what they'll all be doing later don't you, you silly, little garden gnome, you (that thing that sets you to thinking and drinking too much until you swear you're gonna crack in two) when they've all finally paired (and maybe even tripled-) up and gone home and there's just the moon, the garden and you? And the only thing that could possibly be even less relevant than the noxious weeds of a garden gnome's quasi-poetic self pity (that is, to this new world order) is the strange, wild flame of a flower sprouting from a crack in the head of that very gnome, sitting all alone in the corner.

For Some Reason

The night sky is alive tonight
with glittering Diamels
and chittering super-strings
of crickets,

like sleigh bells, almost,
with their near-hypnotic ringing.

And the shadows thrown
from streetlamps are teeming
with these freaky hybrid angel / demon things.

And me, I'm whistling *Do Wah Diddy* in the dark,
stumbling, half-blind, through a graveyard
on my way home from the bar.

And the trees are whispering the latest news
and the grass is strongly advising me to
just lay down and relax.

But hey, there's no time for that
'cause somewhere, out there tonight,
there's a pale, wing'd horse on someone's roof
hoofing out the secret code
for the answers to all our troubles
(or, maybe just the winning lotto numbers).

And there's a weaselly little rat-man
in a long, black coat and top hat
sniffing and prancing about the intersection
of Bedlam and Squalor, calling out,
children, I have lollipops, children!

And a wolf in hobo's clothing
is standing at someone's sub-suburban back door,
inquiring, sheepishly, about a billy goat
or *chosen one* or somethin',

and a sad, sad boy is singin' a curbmouth blues
about a crown that's been seized
by a new king of fools.

And, for some reason, I'm seriously feelin'
like I'm about to be on the business end of some kind
of low-to-mid-level divine judgment (for something
I'm not sure I even did) manifesting itself, maybe,
as a low-hanging tree-limb or slavering set of jaws
charging wildly from out of the dark or old-school
locker-room towel-snap of enlightenment
from The Almighty, Him Self.

And He's urging all his angels and demons alike to
engage target with extreme prejudice!

'Cause the word flittering, moth-like,
through the trees this evening has it that
the Moon has put a price of thirty silver-pieces
on all our fool heads:

those who would dare wander
into her dark garden

without some secret intrigue
to be party to

or some mysterious stranger
to kiss.

Loaded Dice and Poisoned Candy

Hardly even know it's there
most of the time ...

after all, we can be a (somewhat)
fundamentally oblivious species:

whether posited, serenely, in proper lotus position
in the middle of some shimmeringly pristine
mountaintop scenario or deeply steeped
in some sweaty, chaotic configuration of love,

or (just as likely), broke down
on the side of the highway,
I-35 let's say, just south of Topeka, Kansas
(with five pallets of National Enquirers,
bearing the tear-streaked face of Britney Spears,
that has *GOT* to get through):

a weathered cargo ship
run aground under a brutal, relentless sun,
a hundred-and-one in the shade
and a beer can rolling along all of a sudden
like a tumbleweed in an old cowboy movie,
(and now a dog barking off in the distance,
as if on cue).

So, we are allowed, now and then,
an absolution, of sorts,
from our inherent obligation
to fundamental attentiveness
to most of the obvious
and at least some of the finer points
of the subtext, metatext and copious footnotes
to the post, post-modernist novel of *Life*.

But, still *it* hovers and circles,
always lurking just out of the corner of the eye,
waiting for the perfect opportunity to strike,
doling out fate and fortune,
good, bad and indifferent, alike,

the free-floating nucleus
of the all-encompassing,
all-permeating physics of context,
the fluid matrical mechanica
of how things really are,
the constantly shifting locus
of the very *shit* that happens to us,
again and again and again
in sloppy viscous loops ...

The moment ultimately coming to a point,
like the point of a big red arrow
on the Metaphysical Highway
Rest Stop Map Of Life,

like the finger of God pointing,
just a little too accusingly,
at you (and you and you)
as if to say

YOU ARE HERE
(and here you are)!

Hell,
everything else
is extenuating circumstances
and low-grade
accommodation,

loaded dice and poisoned candy.

What *It* Is
(or, That's What I'm Talkin' About!)

It's a feather from the wing
of a naughty Halloween angel.

It's the hot, boozy breath of Kansas;
early evening, late July.

It's flashing red lights waiting for us at the end
of the underground Chunnel Of Lust.

It's the compounding absence that so often
facilitates the eye's reckless wandering,

the drunken sleep of reason
breeding monstrous nightmares
and wicked hangovers of feeling,

the darkness of the deep
Missouri backwoods after sundown
and cellars in abandoned houses
on the edge of town.

It's that high-test grade of silence
that deadens whatever meaningful
thought and speech that might
feasibly arise between us.

It's the fabled philosopher's stone in the soup.
It's bones hauled up from the bottom of a well.
It's snow in the desert (like you would not believe).

We're talking about kickin' the front door in.
We're talking about takin' the back door out.
We're talking a little *body and blood of the Lord,* baby.

We're talking dreams that sparkle and shine
like a tinfoil sculpture or a Roosevelt dime,
like the Czar's crown jewels,
scattered and sewn
out into the backyard
late one night,
like seeds,
like stars,

so they might take root
and grow into whatever it is
they were meant to be.

We're talking about that half-empty glass
of water you brought me

when you know I asked
for gasoline.

Everything Gonna Be All Right (or, Trading Body Blows with the Ghost of Victor Smith)

The night was thick, black and nasty
and my mattress was a raft drifting down
a mighty Mississippi of memory,
a Viking longboat in which my broken
warrior-poet's form had been placed
and sent downstream through the silver-grey mists
of eternity and on to the far bright shores of my
forefathers and their fathers before them,
only to be turned away from those fearsome
gates for being *insufficiently deceased.*

And, lately, it seems like I've been waking up
in the middle of varying stages of dream-state
at all my *former places of residence*, feeling around
the bed for some imaginary *former spouse
or significant other,* freaking out about
being late to some *former place of employment*
and whatever it is I'm gonna say (this time?)
to placate whichever *former employer.*

I can't help but believe if things continue
at this rate, eventually, I'll bolt awake thinking
I'm late for my first day of kindergarten (though,
hopefully my mother will also be on hand to say,
It's OK, little man. It's only Saturday. Go out and play).

And then there's that recurring one where,
in what some new age, metaphysical,
guided meditation counselor type might
call *a deep subterranean cave of me,*
some here-to-fore unknown (or merely suspected)
part of me suddenly cracks and snaps off

like a massive icicle or stalactite, morphing
on its way down into another more fully actualized me,
a new and improved me, you could say,
and hits the ground running like Jesse Owens
at the '36 Olympics.

And let's just say, for the sake of the poem
(and your, most likely, all-too-brief relationship with it),
that this new and improved me is actually you
and it's not a slimy or treacherous cave floor
that your feet have found but a cool, rain-slicked street
late at night in some industrial part of town
you don't recognize.

And just over there to the right,
maybe fifty, sixty feet away at most,
there's a freight train blowing out
its big, brassy *basso profundo*
as it slows down to take the curve
and it's not even an issue of nerve
or wanting it bad enough 'cause you know
you can make it this time, man,
and you don't even have a suitcase
or bag or nothing

but that shit don't even matter 'cause everything's
gonna be different from here on out if you can
just catch that train, man, everything gonna be just fine
if you can just keep runnin' and sayin' it
and sayin' it and sayin' it:

everything gonna be alright,
everything gonna be alright,
everything gonna be alright,
everything ...

Lone Wolves, Black Sheep
and Red-Headed Step-Children

Somewhere,
an empty Mountain Dew bottle
sitting on a limestone fence post
suddenly begins to wheeze and moan
in sweet country harmony
with the wind's sad cowboy song.

Somewhere,
a stiff suburban mummy
stares blankly into his
2,751st consecutive hour
of television;

no one has come calling in years,
no one has noticed the slight,
sickly sweet odor
of wasted irony.

Somewhere, the placid dreams
of a dethroned beauty queen
are stirred by the thought
of stars that died
a million years ago
whose light is just now
reaching us.

And just before dawn,
we'll all be drawn up from
the fathomless well of sleep
to come face to face
with the mongrel faces
of the real *We* ...

the prodigal,
near-primordial hybrid
of the lone wolf,
the black sheep
and the red-headed
stepchild

of which
so many,
half-jokingly,
half-nervously speak.

Psalm #49,
from *The Book of Mean and Evil Truths*
for Josh Rizer

One day, sooner or later,
you will begin to see it:

a memo from the main office
appearing, intermittently, in the classifieds,

on billboards next to highways,
subliminal transmissions
insinuated into the continuum
of prime-time television
and late-night radio programming,

as public service announcements
between infomercials at 3am:

*please find something constructive
to occupy your time.*

Street cleaners and heads of state,
drunken painters, relocated witnesses
and wizened *philosophes*,
they'll all confirm the urgency
of these instructions.

For they too have seen (if but
in their magically realistic dreams, at least),
the Cosmic Steel Toed Boot come swinging.

They know that should you maintain
your current state of in-action,
your current holding pattern of bad faith,
one day, with a long, running start
and supreme universal indifference,

your sweet ass will surely be kicked
right out of the world.

No, not into the void or the here-after, exactly,
not prison or the escape velocity
necessary to achieve a truly perfect madness
(or even the dreaded de-classification
unto the Great American Underclass) ...

but a fate far worse
from which few ever
manage to dig themselves out,
like the final scene from one of those bleak,
existential French or Swedish cinematic dirges
forever looping and repeating itself
again
and again
and again ...

The Great Feast in the grand,
Ayn-Randian dining hall
of the Immortals.

A rickety folding table
set for you in the corner.

A place-card with your name on it
(misspelled, of course).

And there you are,
reeling at the crosshairs of it all,

the guest of the guest of the Guest of Honor,

your demeanor, somewhere between
a boxer's permanent punch-drunk
and low-grade PTSD.

And all the food and booze is gone
and all the lights are out
(except for one dirty bulb
above the sink).

And everyone else
has paired (and even tripled) up
and gone to bed.

And the walls

are thin,

fucko.

(Otherwise) Ridiculous

The lone *Bos primigenius*
on the hill at night,

do you suppose she ever wonders
in her laconic, bovine way
what the stars could possibly be?

Does the *Tyto alba* contemplate
the moon's topography (from his
hayloft perch) or what mysteries might
lay on its darker side?

The *Nephila clavata* centered
in his jeweled web,

does he receive strange frequencies
(or just old radio transmissions)
on its taut wires and filaments?

What about the sleepless *philosopher / poet*
taking his thoughts out for a late-night
walk around the neighborhood?

Does the universe leave cryptic,
fortune-cookie clues and candid
little Polaroids of the *Bigger Picture*
lying around for him to find
and piece together later?

Or is this semi-educated fool merely
adrift on a sea of his own imagining
in the leaky rowboat of his skull

and nothing
but a kerosene lamp,
a stone jug of his uncle's corn liquor
and an old typewriter on which
he may compose

such (otherwise) ridiculous
and impertinent

questions?

Ghosting Around

Tonight,
the sky
is a scarifying movie

and my head
is an empty doll house
(wherein all its (former?)
occupants
are dead).

Yet, instead
of lying quietly
in their places
in the dark
and wormy
Deep
Down,

all these shapes
and faces
keep on bumping
and billowing
and ghosting around
in here somehow.

Yep, there's always
chains a-draggin'
way up there in the attic
where all the leather of bats
and feathery flaps
of crows
are stowed.

Then there's the groanin'
and moanin'
(at two or three
in the mo'nin')
down there in the basement
where the lizards
and crickets
and toads
all go.

And up
and down the stairs,
at rhythmically
confounding intervals,

up and down
the stairs

(sometimes in triplets and pairs),

someone's feets
go stomping

and

clomping.

Still-Life with Catfish, James Brown, Dragon and Freight Train

> *"This aint Bohemia, baby. This is skid row."*
> —Victor Smith

The walls are peeling
and the ceiling is rotting
and the clock in the corner
is chipping away at the night.

And outside, a dog is barking somewhere far off
and someone's shouting down on the street,
HEY RON! HEY RON! IT WASN'T ME, MAN,
IT WASN'T ME!

And the fan on the floor is brushing out a sultry rhythm
and the pipes are whispering all the secrets
of those who've lived here before
and the fridge is humming low,
darlin' do you remember meeee?

And the used car salesman upstairs
is laughing like a mandrill (or crying like a kookaburra),
the people next door, fighting or fucking,
through the walls it's hard to tell.

But through the unlikely collusion
of these people, this place and all the little things
randomly arranged along the winding spectrum in
between, sometimes I think some larger,
more primal thing is trying to contact me.

I have to admit, it's hard to make out most of the time,
like there's just too much metaphysical clutter
or white cosmic noise for the message to get through.

In a painting on the wall, for instance,
a fat catfish is giving the fish-eye
to a hook and worm.

In the corner, sitting on a table,
between a jug of homemade blackberry wine
and a bowl full of nectarines,
the bust of James Brown is eying me
just a little too knowingly,
letting me know with that wicked grin of his
that he's seen everything (and that means *everything!*).

And somewhere, at the bottom
of the deep, murky gravel pit of my gut,
down among the bottles and bones,
the scuttled cars and sunken rowboats,
down among the spiky, prehistoric fish-things
and chitinous mollusks that skulk and sniff about
in the oily dark of this forgotten underworld,
the *Duende* / dragon / angel / demon hybrid
they say lives inside every sensitive artiste type
is tossing and turning again, tossing and turning,
cursing his rotten luck at having been found out again
by the only bigger and badder monstrosity
on the block than him, this accursed,
marauding insomnia that now comes calling
whenever it pleases *(yes it does, whenever it pleases!).*

Though, I know he has been giving
more and more thought,
as time slowly tics and ratchets by,
to raging up in a thunderous,
locomotional flurry of fang and claw
and fire and wing and taking a good-size chunk
out of the ass-end of the world.

Just to see the looks on all our faces.

But outside, up here on the surface of things,
beneath a neo-classical, nocturnal scene
of cirrus clouds and contrails
and a big, bright, mag-light of a moon,
a freight train bound for Talala, OK,
Tucumcari, NM, Ithaca, NY
(or other exotic parts unknown to most of us)
is rumbling its way past the building again,
shaking the very pillars of the earth
like wave after wave of armored cavalry,
rattling the aching frame of Atlas, even ...

How often's it go by, man?

So often you won't even notice.

And Still the Moon

And still the moon
beams down at us
like the atomically radiant skull
of a bald and diabolical clown
with nothing but dark designs
for this sad little town.

And still old grey dreams waft like haunted veils
and shrouds of smoke and steam,
in and out of the boiler room of your soul.

And still the psychotronic call goes out
on lonely, desperate nights
to moths circling streetlights
and stray dogs snuffling
the curb-side garbage
of middle America.

And when the time comes,
the clouds will suddenly grow fat
and sullen as a storm begins to brew
its chunky mulligan stew
of fluster and flurry,
buzzards and crows wings
and the dust and clamor
of a million thundering hooves.

And there, perched on the hill,
just within the weird radiance
of the city's ghostly after-hours glow,
the lone gypsy-prince of coyotes
waits patiently for us, still,

like that near-perfect silence
and stillness of midnight
after the first heavy snow of winter,

like a telegram from beyond the grave
detailing the exact number
of communist spies in the House of Love,

like a recurring nightmare
of a man returned to shore
each morning (alive and well
and only mildly bedraggled)
by an ocean of whiskey
in which he wishes only
to drown the worm
of his sorrow.

Drunk Directing Traffic
at the Intersection of Time and Space

No sooner had I lowered myself
down into that dark well
of ghost echoes and distant whale squeak
than I was the poor boy of every
sad blues and honky-tonk song:

thumb out, on the Lost Highway
and a long, long way from home
(such a long, long way from home),

a lonesome stranger
hoping to hitch a ride
to ever-stranger lands (and
other Parts Unknown, as well).

I was Hank and Lefty,
Kerouac and Cassady,
Quixote and Sancho.

I wore the fabled Hubcap
Diamond-Star Halo and red shoes
that were the envy of every angel
(and devil alike).

I made mid-night raids
on The Garden of Earthly Delights.
I stole Death's pale, raggedy horse
and sold it to a traveling gypsy circus
for pennies on the pound.

I popped, locked and moon-walked
in the middle of traffic
at the intersection of Time and Space.

I rode bitch between a mega-church minister
and a street-corner preacher on a white-knuckle,
cross-country pilgrimage to Nowheresville, USA
(my soon-to-be published account of my adventure
titled, simply, *From East Jesus To Hell's Half Acre
And Back Again: A Hobo's Tale*).

I got drunk on nine kinds of hellfire
and nearly died in a duel
over a one-legged ballerina.

I called out to you through
the dark winter forest of static
at the end of the A.M. radio dial,
waking you in the middle of the night
from dreams of butterflies,
coyotes,
wildflowers ...

If not for the alarm clock
pinching my ear with its
sharp, bony fingers,

I might not have ever made it back.

Standing at the Intersection of Critical Mass and Event Horizon with Tom Wayne and John Deuser, 5:47am (or, *Hey Man, Is That an Accordion I'm Hearing?*)

A million fish wash up dead
in a California harbor.

10,000 cows keel over in Vietnam.

Thousands of Starlings, Turtle Doves
and Red Wing Blackbirds drop from the sky
in Italy, Sweden, South Dakota.

But elsewheres (and despite it all),
we've still managed to put in
another long (and more than respectable) night
of consorting with spirits and keeping
the Universal Kundalini humming
at that slightly heightened pitch (of radians
per reciprocal seconds) which has been
rumored by certain members of the tribe
to induce an *enlightened euphoria* of sorts.

And now the early morning streets (here in mid-town
KC/MO, 5:47am) are strangely Frisco / Portland-foggy
and deserted like one of those old-school / bad dream /
where-did-everybody-go? sci-fi movies from our
paranoid, cold-war era past.

Or so it would seem if not for the all-night diner
with its purple neon *OPEN* sign in the window
and the street light on the corner:

a peach-tinted glow hovering above us
like a stationary UFO whose (only mildly
bemused) occupants are, no-doubt, wondering
if these three zombified monkey-boys
and their fucked up little planet
are even worth the effort.

And from somewhere
deep inside the fog,

a strangely musical

wheezing ...

Charles Simic Sitting in the Cheap Seats of My Dreams

It would appear to be
either a rundown vaudevillian /
burlesque theater, Poughkeepsie
(or Buffalo), NY, circa 19-twenty-something,
or maybe an old, black and white,
*recorded live before a studio
audience* style television program:

part *Honeymooners*,
Days Of Our Lives and
German Expressionist Cinema
consisting almost entirely of various
stock caricatures and other tragi-comic
grotesqueries of the perverse
projectile vomiting hyper-dramatic
dialogue at no one in particular.

They orate, pontificate
and gesticulate, magnificently,
without ever actually seeming to be aware
of each other's existence.

One of them is dressed as a World War I
Prussian military commander,
complete with tall, shiny boots,
walrussy handle bar
and singularly spiked helmet.

Another is, most likely, supposed to be
somebody's *booga-booga* idea of an ancient
tribal shaman or witchdoctor.

Still another, wearing an expensive bra and panties
and a thin silk cord running from his neck to the heel
of the high-heeled shoe on his only remaining foot,
masturbates, dreamily, into the long shadow
of his nightly near-death excursion.

A chorus of mutts and street urchins
waits, attentively, for their cue (or a scrap
of food to fight over, perhaps).

And way in the back,
in the darkest and cheapest of cheap seats,
the lone, cigar smoking audience member
smacks out a slow and clamorous

CLAP!

CLAP!

CLAP!

CLAP!

Chance Meeting, 3am

Well, here we are again,
wandering around in this strangely cool
tide-pool of 3am summertime dark:
just me, myself and my jelly-jar
of green tea and gin, a haunted wind
ruffling its feathers in the trees,
a plastic cup rolling along the street,
and me with a skull like a stone cavern
or shell whispering and roaring with voices
from the past, present and,
very possibly, the future, as well.
There is no one out here to share
the cosmic tragic-comical joke with,
no one to compare notes with,
no one to trade places with, maybe
(if just for a day or two and with
promises made that there'll be no
major crimes committed or persons
fallen in love with), not a solitary neighbor in sight,
not even a front porch light left on
for a flying Dutchman or ancient mariner
lost in the night, not a smoky wisp of a cat
suddenly drifting past or dog with tongue
and tail slappily wagging, not a wayward character
or creature of any kind, not even the chance meeting
of a ghost of some (recently deceased) second cousin
(on my mother's side).

Madame Laveau, Fortune Teller and Police Psychic, Begins to See the Light

Somewhere, out there, in this bleak,
little Romanian opera of a city
full of feral cats, rusted iron
and restless spirits steaming up
from sewer grates is a blind man
selling Nightingales,

an accordion wheezing out
a sad, meandering tune
from deep within the inner-most
recesses of strange shadows,

a wind-up submarine
marooned at the bottom
of a cast-iron tub (with three
gnarled feet and a brick
subbing in for the missing fourth),

a Punch and Judy puppet show
starring Mickey Mouse
and Marlene Dietrich,

a black votive candle (dedicated
to some lesser known saint) burning
with a blue flame in a 3rd story window,

a barn owl perched on a flag pole,

Kafka playing deep chess with a bed bug,

Tennessee Williams making small talk with an iguana,

a billy goat munching on a page
from *Being And Nothingness,*

a silver-grey cat napping
on the bar of a hotel cabaret,
a New Year's Eve streamer (from exactly
fifteen years before) hanging
from the ceiling, almost all the way
down to the floor,

a man sitting at a table in the corner,
sipping Sambuca and soda (fleeting thoughts
of his youth like showers of shooting stars
raking across his mind),

smoke from a stubbed-out cigarette
coiling up through a red-orange spotlight,
shining down on a tragic torch singer type
who has suddenly forgotten the words
to a song she's sung a thousand times before.

And hey,
have you heard the one
about the plumber
and the midget
transvestite?

Madame Laveau, Fortune Teller and Police Psychic, Hands Out a Little Free Advice

To come upon a red guitar
propped in the corner of an empty room
at that exact point in the day when afternoon
is, officially, about to shift into evening
means you will soon be embroiled
in a scandal with a blue-eyed girl.

To dream of an elevator shaft
coughing up an ocean of blood is a sign
that someone close to you, maybe even family,
is plotting your downfall.

A noose swinging from a tree on a hill
means you will marry many times
before you find the right one.

A beer bottle standing in the middle
of a country crossroads means that a decision
of some importance must soon be made.

To dream, repeatedly, of a votive candle
burning in an attic bedroom window
means you will soon change religions,
political parties or the color of your hair.

To wake from a dream of washing dishes
and find yourself washing dishes is a sign
that you are about to receive a large inheritance.

To see a telephone pole by the side of the road
suddenly begin to shoot sparks and billow with smoke
means that you will soon encounter temptation
you might not be able to fend off.

To see the face of your enemy
in the skin of a potato, in a bank
of clouds or looking up at you
from the coffee in your cup means
you should probably keep
a low profile for awhile.

To find a reproduction of an ancient map
of pre-iceage Antarctica
folded up in the pages of a book
on seventeenth century French painters
means you will soon begin a strange journey
with someone you haven't spoken to in years.

The Story, So Far
with apologies to Arthur Tress

It all starts with a young Adam West and Eva Gabor
(having been cast, here, as a sort of flawlessly wholesome
American Hansel and Gretel) gathering up sheaves
of wheat in the purple-orange after-glow of a setting sun,
the whole thing set to a lush accompaniment of angels
with Chinese eyes playing strange, other-worldly
instruments.

And now a tongueless dwarf (with a bright-feathered bird
perched on his shoulder) is standing by the side of the road,
holding, in one hand, the keys to a Chevy van (with a
valkyrie / viking princess air-brushed on the sides) and a
stained and tattered road atlas in the other.

And Johnny Socko and Giant Robot are finally done with
their daring-do adventuring for another day (having
saved the day, once again, from the clutches of the evil
Professor Hex and the Dragon Lady from Mars) and are
now slowly spiraling down into a deep and
dreamless sleep.

And Caruso, reviving his most famous role in *Pagliacci*,
is giving voice lessons to Anne Boleyn (or is it Jane
Mansfield?) while some bit-part player (you know you've
seen her a million times, before) done-up in cliché
antebellum slave-girl garb is grinning a near-rictus grin
and beating out a jungle beat on an old washtub
and a tambourine.

And all the while an (as yet) unidentified goddess
or muse waits, anxiously, in the wings for her cue.

And it's hotter than a Mexican sidewalk.

And Time is slouching, leisurely,
like some rough, lazy beast
toward the capitol city-state of The Self.

And that crazy *sumbitch* Sisyphus
has had his sentence re-commuted (once again)
to splitting cunt hairs with Ockham's razor
for all eternity (or just the fore-seeable duration).

And all the while,
a butterfly sits dreaming on a railroad spike:
a dream of suddenly waking from a dream
and finding oneself to be nothing less
than The Great American Everyman, himself,
who (it will eventually be revealed
through a succession of wildly improbable events)
has somehow come into possession
(one could very easily name it either a curse
or a blessing) of a magical toy chicken
that lays chocolate eggs covered in 14K gold leaf.

No one could possibly predict what happens next
or how the whole thing
finally ends.

Chet Baker Begins to Bleed

There's grinning ghost-poets
riding fancy saddles
down abandoned hotel hallways,

a red rooster
wrestling a baby Kingsnake,

a cat caught in the hen house
and a shiftless, no-good drifter
cooling in the jailhouse.

There's a broken-down truck
afloat on an ocean of golden wheat
beneath a swirling coal-black sky.

There's a foolish old rowboat
sulking in the bed of a creek
that's long since run dry
(still waiting after all these years
for the creek to reappear).

And here's the part
where one of our own dearly departed
is carried down an inner-city street
on a swollen river of laughter and tears,
trumpets, tambourines and slide trombones,
farther and farther out, towards some still (as yet)
greater unknown.

And what about that mad Rasputin of a character
down in his subterranean lair,
sculpting zodiac animals from spirits
of fire and air?

And way up there, just above the city skyline,
goes the Man With All The Answers,
wafting away to some faraway land, most likely,
on a *deus ex machina* made of wanderlust,
bailing wire and gull's wings,

leaving us a world of mysteries
that may very well remain unanswered
forever more (*forever more ... forever more ...*)

But then, before anyone can catch their breath, even,
comes the big budget / *WHAMMO!* / climactic scene
where the stadium floor of the world's latest
collective dream (of whatever's passing, these days,
for peace, love and understanding) suddenly blows
and drops out from beneath it all

and we tumble and fall,
tumble and fall,
tumble and fall,

like starfish,
like rag dolls,
like satellites spiraling, drunkenly,
out of their orbits,
off into the sleepy, wakening yawn
of a shimmering nebula, the stellar semblance
of a giant rose a million years wide
and the color of peach ice cream.

Somewhere, a pay phone
by the side of a desert highway
begins to ring.

Somewhere, a tattoo of Chet Baker
begins to bleed.

Sleep During Thunderstorms

The quality of sleep during thunderstorms
((not wholly un-)like that which is to be had
in hammocks on late Spring days
but instead, of course, with the obligatory
wind and rain howling and pounding away
at the house (if not the very foundations
of the earth itself)) always seems
to free the sleeper to sink
deeper and deeper down
to those primal subterranean layers
of semi-consciousness where sleep
is more like a ghostly oceanic underworld
and dreams are luminescent fish
skulking about among the weeds
and abandoned machines and whatever
other random little trinkets and forgotten things
that filter their way down there from the surface world,
down and down through the hundreds
and thousands of pounds per cubic inch.
And, sometimes, you suddenly come awake
down there inside the belly of a dream,
just lilting along on whatever
under-current that comes sliding by.
And, though you've become slightly
more self-aware (of a few of your
other selves) down there in the briny,
dreamy deep-down,
you do not
drown.

Ghost Out Wandering the Backroads
(or, John Brown Returns to Kansas)

There are plenty of paintings
and a few photographs, even,
so we know someone
fitting his description
once moved amongst us
and has allegedly been witnessed,
recently, slipping in and out of
the fitful dreams of the CEOs, holy men
and politicians of Kansas (running guerrilla raids
and counting coup, no doubt).

They appear to us somehow more shifty,
nervous and disingenuous than usual
and, reportedly, state-wide sales
of expensive scotches, designer anti-depressants
and blood-pressure medications are through the roof.

They say he observes them often from the tree-line
behind their palatial guest houses,
from bus-stop benches down on the street
across from their office parks and complexes,
from over their shoulders in the mirrors
of exclusive country club and executive washrooms:

his eyes like signal fires on distant hilltops,
like lanterns leading us through swamps and hollers
and piney backwoods on up to Freedomland *(glory be!)*,
like Klieg lights calmly surveying and laying open
the meat-processing plants and voting stations
and payday loan offices and publicly subsidized
million-dollar mega-farms and mega-churches
of the over-worked, under-paid, trans-fattened heart
of The Heartland.

He has no visible means of transportation;
he is always just suddenly there and then
just as suddenly not there,
and certainly doesn't possess
quite the ferocious bearing and terrifying
tornadic stature transmitted to us over the years
by Curry's paintings in the state capitol building.

Yet, there is always a quicksilver halo
of ghost fire around him,
a layer of graveyard mud on his boots
and an expertly tied noose
(with exactly thirteen knots)
hanging from his neck.

And when the time inevitably comes
to raise the question of what
it could all possibly mean,
everyone of these generous job creationists,
these steely admirals of the fleets of industry,
these selfless stewards of the souls of men,
suddenly seems to scurry away to some
dust-bowl era storm cellar
somewhere deep within themselves,

while their eyes try to focus
on some distant flittering thing
on the far, fabled horizon
of whatever's left of the 21st century
American dream.

What Else to Do?
with deepest apologies to the ghosts of Li Po, Tu Fu and Su Tung-po

Night, and the first few tentative drops
of a much-needed and long-prayed-for
summer rain going *plip, plip, plip*
down through the trees' many
cross-hatched layers of branches and leaves
to the summer-hot sidewalk below,

the trees like tattered beach umbrellas
sprouting, here and there, along the banks
of this lazy river of newly-laid tarmac,

a shy ghost in the attic window across the street,
tiny voices in the wind and grass
whispering choruses of praise (each to each)
to the Grand Schemata Of Peoples / Places / Things,
the micro-cosmic minutia of it all and all other
various originators of little and large moments
of deep enlightenment, in between.

And here I am (again, it seems),
legs in *faux* lotus position, at the epicenter
of who knows how many known,
unknown and very possibly unknowable
spheres and ellipses of influence.

What else to do, then,
but raise my pint bottle up to the grinning,
blue Buddha moon to catch a view of him
through the brandy's amber luminescence
and the streaming, CinemaScopic projection
of clouds against the sky, and salute
his blissed-out, other-worldly magnificence?

My skeleton is an aching
abstract construct.

My heart is an old,
abandoned country church.

My mind is a flickering street light
at the heart of a feathery flurry
of poems that may never be finished.

Midnight on the Eighteenth Hole
at the *Club Purgatorio*

We
have finally reached
the swampy inland sea of
late June where a newly-minted
silver-dollar moon has illuminated all the
plumes and scattered wings and wind-blown
drapes of cloud that have accumulated on the ceiling of the
Royal Blue dome of heaven, drawing all their static and coin to
the surface from the deep wells of their dark and turbulent hearts.

And all the trilling, tremoloing tree frogs and basso-belching bull
frogs are out cutting heads in full force, tonight, volleying
their tribal haka and hoodoo tunes, back and forth,
across this swollen, marshy pond, from which
the giant, cyclopean over-lord of some
alternate, inversely mirrored
underworld peers out
with a single bright
eye.

Head Full of Boogeymen / Belly Full of Snakes (or, No Escape from the Island of Misfit Boyz)

Some nights,
the restless specter of the mind
will just not lie still,
opting instead to skulk about
the dark, Gothic country-side of the psyche:
the foggy moors of the emotions,
the primeval backwoods of pre-historic memory,
the two-lane highways and old back-roads,
like stitches, criss-crossing and holding
the whole gooey, grey mass together.

On nights like these,
when the flesh (and perhaps the ego, as well)
is bruised and battered beyond recognition,
and the ancient, haunted scaffolding of the bones
is creaking and popping,
like an old cedar tree in the wind,
under the compounded and constantly shifting weight
of the 60-hour work week,

when the sprawling network of nerves and arteries
and capillaries is a NASCAR speedway (enriched by
high-octane coffee and toxic energy drinks),

it's then that the spirit searches, longingly,
for a co-sponsor, of sorts,
a technical advisor or low-grade savior, even,
to shepherd us through yet another
shadowy valley of sleepless Summer hell,

an intermediary between the cold, indifferent cosmos
and the unreconstructed cave dweller that still huddles,
fearfully, somewhere inside us all.

We're talking one of those nights of endless,
sexistential free-fall into the gaping, black maw
of the great Space / Time consortium,
like a city-block-sized sink-hole
just suddenly opened up beneath you,

deep and dark as the legendary
long, dark tunnel of the soul
(about which, so many poems
and stories and songs are so earnestly
purged out into the wild, blue
meme-o-sphere every year).

But here, the light at the end
is the light leaking out
from the other side of a door
left cracked open, conveniently, for you
(almost as if someone were expecting you):

a light with the weird luminescence of the light
one would dig one's own grave by, maybe,
or better yet, a prison break light
or concentration of multi-colored spot lights
shining down on you at that precise precarious moment
you've forgotten the lines to your big,
solemn, earnest speech to Life's unsmiling
and wildly indifferent grand jury.

And despite what half the ghosts in your head
and damn near every one of the snakes in your belly
are telling you, you proceed, heedlessly, anyway ...

only to bolt awake, 4:37am,
some place you don't recognize,
an old-fashioned rotary-dial telephone *ringing*
and *ringing* like a goddamn ice-pick in your ear,

a collect-call from the Island Of Misfit Boyz,
it seems,

a Mr. Charley In The Box
(yeah, you remember,
you guys go *waaaay* back)

and will you accept
the charges?

Weathervane Creaking in a Sad, Grey Wind
(or, a Secret History of the Nighttime World)

There's a weathervane creaking
in a sad, grey wind.

Buzzards spiraling on an invisible whirlpool
of Brownian motion, winding deeper and deeper
down to the bottom of night's mysterious inland sea.

A bed-side radio channeling old transmissions
of The Shadow, The Lone Ranger
and Little Orphan Annie,
pulling street sweepers, star quarter-backs
and bank presidents alike
back into the shallow end of sleep.

A man stepping out of the side door of his life
and into a waiting pick-up truck,
then down to the corner convenience store
for a liter of vodka and a carton of cigarettes,
(never to return).

A mysterious strain of fortune cookies
giving the fragmented (but true), play-by-play account
of what really went down at Golgotha, Wounded Knee,
Nan King, Roanoke, Roswell, Ferguson.

A bald eagle perched on a stop light
at the corner of 39th and Bell,
KC/MO, 64111, 9:43 pm, Tuesday.

A pocket watch ticking on the end of a chain,
hanging from the rear-view mirror
of a '62 purple Impala (suicide doors,
peek-a-boo lights, Buddha on the dash-board).

A hobo sleeping in a rowboat
in a dried-up creek bed
beneath the white rose
of a cemetery moon.

A rusty railroad spike driven through
a heart-shaped box of candy, left on the front porch
of one who has not been true *(you know what you did)*.

Two freight trains passing in a foggy train yard,
like ships in a harbor, then back out
onto the high seas of the lower Midwest.

A street corner crazy
giving God and the Devil, both,
a little dose of the old *what for*.

An unknown number of
feral cats revving themselves up
to either fight or fuck.

And all the while,
a lone, melancholy moon-moth of a thought
flutters and bounces around inside
the empty Victorian opera house
of some old man's skull,
settles for a moment,
then goes back
to its manic gypsy dance
before he can catch it.

What Is *It*, This Time?

What is it, this time?

It's a set of elevator doors,
endlessly and randomly opening and closing
on all our various levels of perception /
consciousness / awareness / etc.

It's a slippery gateway drug
down a long helical flight
of ever-expanding co-dependencies.

It's an attic window lit with a mysterious glow
in a house where no one has lived for years
(where many a secret passageway
is rumored to silently serpentine).

What is it, this time!?

It's a hairpin turn in an already labyrinthine path
through the Garden of Earthly Delights.

It's an epic poem
folded into a leaky haiku of a boat
then set afloat on a lazy, meandering meme-stream
that runs (mostly unnoticed) through all our lives.

It's a deep, drunken mid-day nap,
ended suddenly by a dream of wind
and thunder and a violent knocking
at the back door (to which you stumble
clumsily and frantically
only to find no one there).

What is it, this time!!?

It's a midnight rendezvous
with Fate, Karma, Kismet and Assoc.

It's a June Bug struggling
on the floor of a bath tub
in an abandoned motel
by the side of a road you really,
really don't want to go down.

It's a long, deep sigh let loose
like the last leaf of a dead tree
on to the frozen surface of a kiddie pool.

It's a rotting tree limb finally cracking
and falling from the accumulated weight and misery
of an ancient hangman's noose in a forest
of tall, creaking skeletons and perpetual fog
in which too many people have been hung.

What is it, this time!!!?
It's the lone gypsy prince of coyotes
calling up the spirits of his dead ancestors
for one last suicidal reunion tour
before the Big Bad Ragnarok*
of so many late-night campfire tales
inevitably comes rumbling, tumbling down.

It's a train broke down in a tunnel
with no light at the end.

What is it, this time!!!!?

Let me tell you what it is, *cha-cha*,
on the house and country simple,
so listen up and get it straight.

It's a priest crying with laughter
at a joke his friend the rabbi has told him
about a priest, a rabbi and a donkey
who walk into a Bar Mitzvah.

That's what it is.

Asshole.

*Ragnarok — *In Norse mythology, a series of future events, including a great battle, foretold to ultimately result in the death of a number of major figures (including the gods Odin, Thor, Týr, Freyr, Heimdallr, and Loki), the occurrence of various natural disasters, and the subsequent submersion of the world in water.*

You Are Here: A Meditation on Phenomenology and Spiritualism (with a Side of Jalapeños and Mezcal)
for Michael Morales

Whereas
                I'm not so much
     a full-on, absolute *denier,*
           but really more of what you might call a
                methodological
                            naturalist /
        soft-hearted atheist /
     hard-nosed agnostic (with gnostically
                      paganish proclivities
          and a soft spot
     for the weird, fanciful and mysterious)
            when it comes to matters concerning
supernatural phenomena / spirit worlds /
                higher powers / etc., etc.,
     but if I were more
     hard-wired that way (if not exactly
a full-on true believer)
                and if my ratio
          of wiring to whatever quantifiable level
of good old fashioned
            common credulity
     were to extend to the idea of actually
communing with and / or summoning
     said supernatural phenomena /
                        spirit worlds /
     higher powers / etc., etc., then I'd have to say
that two men of (otherwise)
                  sound mind
          sitting across a table from one another
(*mano a mano,* as if locked in a fierce war of wills
     on the psychic plain),

consuming raw slices
                    of jalapeños and
                    washing them down with shots of
            mezcal (*con gusano,* by the way,
    if that makes any difference, though I don't
                    know why it would) would
    probably be as effective a *deus ex machina*
        as any for calling down the weird lightning
of mystic visions
                        and prophetic dreams
            and very possibly setting the cosmic
        revolving door (that is rumored to exist),
                between this world and who knows
    how many others,
                    to spinning like
                            a roulette wheel on which
        the little black ball of the mind
                                (the black pearl
                of all potential and / or accumulated
    human knowledge and wisdom)
            must eventually,
                        inevitably come to a rest

                    (if but for
                            the moment).

Return of *It*

Maybe from under my pork-pie hat
like an explosion of butterflies and confetti

or from under the shadowy eave
of a barn like a squall of Starlings
taking to the sky,

or, from the far side
of the mysterious *Planet X*, even
(rumored to orbit the fading campfire
of our little solar system,
like a black ghost that stays, always,
just beyond the reach of its light),

or maybe, just this instant,
fallen from the pages of a book
on arc-welding

or hopping, leap-frog-like, from a cigar-box
found beneath the floorboards
of an empty apartment
in downtown Sturgeon Bay.

Most likely, though, It comes
from that flickering nexus between 1 and -1,
between blind faith and forbidden knowledge,
between the could have
and the *Goddamn, I should have!*

But, recent studies are showing there's a strong chance
that It claws itself up each night from a shallow grave
that, years ago, It was forced, at gunpoint, to dig.

Though, rumors have been circulating
that It's available, exclusively,
through a mysterious import / export company
whose adds appear only in old copies
of *Club Magazine, Famous Monsters of Filmland*
and *The Savage Sword of Conan* (#s 134-151).

Maybe It's reordering someone's
prize baseball card or record collection
right this dark and stormy minute,
by the light of a dirty bulb
in an attic bedroom
that no one has been home to
in years.

Or maybe It's down in the kitchen,
napping in the lonely gap between
a glass of Old Charter, 10 Year,
and a book by Erle Stanley Gardner
(or is it the immortal Zane Grey?).

It flutters, moth-like, from dark corners
with impossible geometries
and the pockets of old tuxedos
in Goodwill stores,

from the yawning mailboxes
of abandoned farm houses,
from the trunks of cars
scuttled to the bottoms
of backwoods ponds,

from the jaws of skeletons
locked in closets
for telling unbelievable truths.

It crosses mind-blowing metaphysical distances
just to blow a sad little tune
across the dusty mouths of old beer bottles
sitting on fence posts or front porch steps,

or to throw itself, selflessly,
in front of an oncoming taxi
or east-bound Greyhound bus

so that some damn fool
(maybe even you)
may live at least one more day

to write poems,
pick flowers
or play video games.

With Its last dying breath It rasps,

Choose wisely.

ACKNOWLEDGMENTS

Thanks to the editors of the following publications where (versions of) the poems in this book originally appeared:

The Smoking Poet, The Gloom Cupboard, On The Inside, Duct Tape And Coffin Nails, Poetry Bay, The Poetry Warrior, Gutter Eloquence, Hobo Camp Review, Common Line Project, Dream International Quarterly, Main Street Rag, Alternative Reel, Handful Of Dust, Eviscerator Heaven, Clockwise Cat, Killpoet, Carcinogenic Poetry, Up The Staircase Quarterly, Guerrilla Pamphlets, The Meth Lab, Inclement, Dark Lady Poetry, b. ak. Tun magazine, Horror Sleaze Trash, As Well As Magazine, Protected: Poetry of Trains, Ann Arbor Review, Citizens for Decent Literature, Thunder Sandwich, Mid-Western Gothic, Message In A Bottle, Off Beat Pulp, Bluest Aye, The Screech Owl, Faircloth Review, and *Words Dance.*

Special thanks to the following:

39 West Press, Prospero's Books, The Fellowship of N-finite Jest and all the 39th Street Irregulars, Will Leathem, Riley Leathem, Tom Wayne, Amy Giblin, Jeanette Powers, Brandon Whitehead, Jon Bidwell, John Deuser, j.d.tulloch, Shawn Pavey, Steven H. Bridgens, Ezhno Martin, Jason Preu, Kelsey Snow, Margeruite Rappold, Mark Hennessy, Kevin Rabas, Al Ortolani, George Wallace, Jameson Bayles, John Dorsey, Mark McClane, Greg Edmondson, and the whole OAC Road Team.

Jason Ryberg is the author of twelve books of poetry, six screenplays, a few short stories, several angry letters to various magazine and newspaper editors, and a box full of folders, notebooks and scraps of paper that could one day be (loosely) construed as a novel. He is currently an artist-in-residence at both The Prospero Institute of Disquieted P/o/e/t/i/c/s and the Osage Arts Community. He lives part-time in Kansas City, with a rooster named Little Red and a billy goat named Giuseppe, and part-time somewhere in the Ozarks, near the Gasconade River, where there are also many strange and wonderful woodland critters.

www.ingramcontent.com/pod-product-compliance
Lightning Source LLC
Chambersburg PA
CBHW021442080526
44588CB00009B/640